TABLE O

PART III
RESOURCES TOOLKIT

INTRO

"As an actor, you are in a unique position because you're not only memorizing dialogue but really embodying it. You naturally feel the rhythm of good writing."
– Jesse Eisenberg

Great dialogue not only entertains but also builds conflict, increases tension, propels the story forward, and reveals character and theme. You've probably heard this before. However, it can a very tricky thing for aspiring screenwriters to pull off because we often tend to approach dialogue as just "characters talking." But it isn't... On the one hand dialogue needs to feel casual and "real," just like how people talk in real life. But on the other hand, movie dialogue isn't how people talk in real life at all. Instead, it's a heightened reality in which people hardly ever stumble over their words or go off-track, are much wittier than usual and always know just the right thing to say at just the right time. The trick, then, is in making dialogue *feel like real life*, but with every single word chosen for a reason and earning its place in the script.

Please note: this book probably won't elevate your screenplay dialogue to a level found in *Casablanca* overnight. What it will do, however, is get your dialogue working *for* your script rather than against it, through a series of Theory Hacks and Practical Exercises designed to combat the common pitfalls aspiring screenwriters fall into when it comes to characters' conversations.

Before we start, we'd like to dispel some of the myths surrounding dialogue—that it's somehow a bad thing that should always be cut in favor of an image. The "show don't tell" advice usually goes something like this: "Film is 80 percent visual and 20 percent audio, so you must always use pictures over words. If your script was turned into a silent film, we should still be able to follow what's going on." While true to a point, this advice is misleading because it fails to account for the fact that if you put on any movie at random, chances are you'll land on a conversation, not a silent scene or image.

The problem with this advice is that it implies all dialogue is "un-cinematic." It implies Tarantino shouldn't have opened Pulp Fiction on a long conversation between Pumpkin and Honey Bunny in a diner, but instead on them immediately sticking up the place. Likewise, maybe Jon Favreau shouldn't have opened *Swingers* on Mike sat opposite Rob in a diner, but instead on him standing outside his ex-girlfriend's apartment in the rain calling up to her window.

There is, of course, certainly a place for implementing the "show don't tell" maxim within scenes, which we'll get into later. Sometimes it's better to show a character's intention or emotion through action rather than dialogue, or by writing a whole scene with little or no dialogue. But if you want to become a screenwriter, you're going to have to learn how to push scenes forward through the characters' conversations as well as images.

In order to help you do this, we've broken down the three most common mistakes aspiring screenwriters make regarding dialogue, and provided a Theory Hack and a Practical Exercise designed to combat each one.

Firstly, here are the three most common problems:

1. Too much dialogue. Characters ramble, hold speeches and generally waffle on about things with no purpose.

2. Conversations feel clunky, unnatural, cheesy, expository, or what is often referred to as "on-the-nose."

3. All the dialogue sounds the same. No matter who's speaking, every character sounds suspiciously like the writer.

Eliminate all three of these problem areas from your characters' dialogue by implementing the techniques in this book—as well as other exercises designed to elevate their speech—and you'll be well on your way to crafting screenplay dialogue that's up there with the pros.

THEORY HACKS

"Let your characters talk to each other and do things. Spend time with them—they'll tell you who they are and what they're up to."
– Greta Gerwig

Let's get started with three great Theory Hacks that will show how to avoid the three most common mistakes found in spec scripts and what to do instead.

HACK I: CUT THROUGH THE TREES

How do you know if you're overwriting your dialogue? And how can you tackle it if you are? As we've already mentioned, you've probably heard that if the dialogue isn't revealing character or pushing the story forward, it can be cut. While this may be easy to understand intellectually, it can often be hard to implement in a script when you're deep in the story and want to let the characters talk as much as they want.

In other words, it can be hard to tell the difference between effective dialogue that deserves to be in a script and general chit-chat that doesn't. The latter often results in dialogue that runs long, with characters making speeches or just sitting around shooting the breeze, and this means you're overwriting it. When dialogue stretches to four or five lines or more, or is just a friendly conflict-free conversation, it might not seem like a problem when you're writing it, but it really drags on screen.

While the advice to "cut any dialogue that doesn't reveal character or move the story forward" is true, we think it's easier to achieve this if you approach it from the perspective of characters engaged in a battle.

TENNIS, ANYONE?

The best moments of dialogue often come between two characters who are at odds with each other—when they're using their words like weapons. Or in the case of this analogy—tennis racquets. A great way to edit a conversation and also inject some conflict and stakes into it, is to think of it as a game of tennis. Particularly in confrontational scenes, there should be a sense in the characters' dialogue that they're struggling to make the other realize something important. That they're taking it in turns playing defensive or attacking shots while trying to get the upper hand over the other. And that their words are putting each other under tremendous pressure and causing a great deal of stress.

Rather than thinking of dialogue in casual conversational terms, try to think of it as a tennis game between the characters—each one hitting the ball across the net with a line that tops the last, until finally one hits the "winner." Here's an example from the film *The Girl On The Train*. This is the scene in which the protagonist, Rachel, is confronted by Detective Riley over whether or not she killed her neighbor. Note how the dialogue resembles a battle between these two characters, until finally Riley wins the "game" with the line, "Did you murder Megan Hipwell?"

INT. POLICE BATHROOM - MOMENTS LATER

Riley opens the door of a police station bathroom and signals Rachel inside.

Riley crosses to the sink and looks into the mirror above it for a long beat. Uneasy, Rachel walks towards Riley.

> RILEY
> You wanted to file a statement? I'm listening. [SERVE]

> RACHEL
> Scott Hipwell just assaulted me. [DEFENSIVE RETURN]

> RILEY
> You mean your new boyfriend Scott Hipwell? [ATTACKING SHOT]

> RACHEL
> No. We were just friends. [DEFENSIVE RETURN]

> RILEY
> But that's what you wanted, isn't it? I mean, you got him to stay overnight at your apartment, right? [ATTACKING SHOT]

> RACHEL
> No. You need... You need the context. [DEFENSIVE RETURN]

Riley turns from the mirror and approaches.

RILEY
I know the context. But what I'm
trying to determine is when your
obsession with Mr. Hipwell began.
Was it before or after his pregnant
wife was murdered? I mean, you were
neighbors at one point?
[ATTACKING SHOT]

RACHEL
I met him after...
[DEFENSIVE RETURN]

RILEY
After being questioned by me, you
befriend another even more obvious
suspect than yourself, and then you
manage to get him to incriminate
himself all the while hoping he'll
fuck you. [ATTACKING SHOT]

RACHEL
I came here trying to help you. He
just assaulted me in my own house!
[ATTACKING SHOT]

RILEY
You were seen in the area that
night. There are several hours that
you say you can't account for.
[ATTACKING SHOT]

This is news to Rachel. Her resolve begins to unsettle.

RACHEL
It was Scott. Scott Hipwell killed
his wife. [DEFENSIVE RETURN]

                    RILEY
        No. He didn't. Surveillance footage
        from a sports bar accounts for Mr.
        Hipwell's whereabouts that night.
        [ATTACKING SHOT]

She moves in, quietly insistent.

                    RILEY
        You're lying. You're lying.
        [ATTACKING SHOT]

Rachel is terrified. Riley puts a comforting hand on her arm.

                    RILEY
        Tell me what happened. It's okay.
        Tell me. [ATTACKING SHOT]

                    RACHEL
        I don't know... [DEFENSIVE RETURN]

Riley leans in close to Rachel's face. She's calm.

                    RILEY
        Did you murder Megan Hipwell?
        [WINNING SHOT]

A moment. Rachel realizes she doesn't know the answer. She
flees in a panic.

See how there's no room for waffle here? And how every
single line is included for a reason because it's either an
attacking shot or defensive return over the net.

Of course, not every conversation in a movie is a full-on
confrontation that moves the plot forward, comparable to

game of tennis. Sometimes dialogue can be very low key, friendly, and only reveal character or backstory. Take a look at the scene in *Wild* in which Cheryl meets another female hiker on the trail and all they do is chat about their lives. Or the scene in *The Way, Way Back* in which the teenage protagonist, Duncan, has his first proper conversation with the girl next door, Susanna. Or the one in *The Skeleton Twins* in which Maggie and Milo sit on the floor talking about high school. While the tennis game analogy might not fit these kind of scenes, if the *balance of conversations* in your script resemble conflict-free exchanges rather than battles in which they're both vying to get the upper hand, then you probably have a lack of conflict in the story overall.

In this case, reframing the dialogue as a game of tennis—with each character playing defensive or attacking shots—can really help add some pressure, conflict and stakes. In turn, this will help stop characters chatting for the sake of it, as you'll be forced to focus the dialogue only on what's important.

QUICK WIN EDITS

When a character talks about something for half a page it's not as interesting as finding just the exact right words for them to say in two lines. The art of writing tight dialogue is taking what can be said in fifty words and then cutting it down to forty. And then to thirty. And then to twenty. And so on. This helps keep the dialogue flowing and as interesting (and realistic) as possible. Next time you watch a movie, pay particular attention to how little each character says all in one go. You will find that it's hardly any time at all before another character's speaking.

With that in mind, here are some quick win edits that will help immediately tighten up your dialogue. Use Cmd+F to highlight each character's name and tab through all their dialogue looking for examples of the bad habits below:

1. Dialogue over three lines. Start by applying the "three lines or less" rule. If any characters are speaking for more than three lines, see if they can be cut. Then once they're down to three lines see if you can cut them down to two, and so on. Less is most definitely more when it comes to screenplay dialogue.

2. Repetition. "I'm done helping you! No more. That's it. You won't get any more help from me." This is overwriting because we only need to hear a character express an idea once to get it. Just leave in the one essential point of what a character needs to say. In this case, "I'm done helping you!" would probably suffice.

3. Goodbyes and hellos. "Hi, Matt. How are you? Hi, Sarah. I'm fine thanks. How are you?" It's possible to get to the "meat" of the scene much quicker by cutting many instances of characters saying goodbye or hello to each other.

4. Full sentences. Try to resist writing out full sentences in characters' dialogue as this can not only make it run long, but also come off as overly formal. "Would you mind showing me how to get there, please?" could be, "Can you show me?" Or just, "Show me?"

5. Lack of interruptions. When characters interrupt each other and trail off at the ends of sentences it not only saves space but feels more realistic. For example, "I guess I could let you have the blue one. But you do know that's my lucky color?" "Yes, yes, I know. Just give it here." This could be edited down to, "I guess I could, but..." "Give it here."

6. Telegraphing action. Try cutting down instances of a character saying they're going to do something and then showing them go ahead and do it. There's often no need to have a character say, "I'm going to make a chicken sandwich," and then show them go make a chicken sandwich. Similarly, most instances of characters making plans—say, meeting at a bar—can be cut and just replaced by opening the scene with everyone already there, mid-conversation.

HACK II: GET OFF-THE-NOSE

On-the-nose dialogue is probably the closest thing to Kryptonite to be found in a spec screenplay. This is primarily because it's not how people talk in real life. It feels fake—and if what your characters say feels fake, everything about the scene feels fake as well. In this section we're going to take a look at what on-the-nose dialogue actually is, how to root out and, most importantly, how to turn it into realistic, professional quality dialogue.

WHAT IS ON-THE-NOSE DIALOGUE?

When dialogue is described as "on-the-nose" it means it doesn't feel true to the characters—usually because they're explaining things in an overly simplistic way for the benefit of the reader, rather than how they'd naturally talk among themselves.

Here's an example from a spec screenplay of on-the-nose dialogue between two friends that we'll be referring back to throughout the section:

INT. KATIE'S BEDROOM - DAY

Katie and Jennifer are sitting on the bed.

> JENNIFER
> I take it you didn't get the part
> in that sitcom?

> KATIE
> They didn't even let me audition.

> JENNIFER
> Did you ever think about taking
> acting lessons?

> KATIE
> Yes, but acting lessons cost money,
> which I don't have.

> JENNIFER
> Can't you borrow some from your
> parents?

> KATIE
> Yeah right. That's not gonna happen.

JENNIFER
What are you going to do?

KATIE
I don't know. I feel so helpless.
My life's a mess!

Note not only how unrealistic and uninteresting this conversation feels, but the way it screams from the page, "Hey, I'm an amateur writer." It's a tough skill to master (even professional screenwriters get pulled up on this one) but before we get to how to edit stilted dialogue like this, let's take a look at how to find it in the first place.

HOW TO RECOGNIZE ON-THE-NOSE DIALOGUE

"Use irony," "Show don't tell," "What's *not* said is more important than what *is* said," etc. have to be some of the most oft-repeated pieces of screenwriting advice out there, and yet they can be hard to put it into practice if you're too wrapped up in your own story to be able to recognize it in the first place.

Use the two methods below to weed out clunky dialogue:

1. The question mark test. Hit Cmd + F on your keyboard, pop a question mark symbol in the search field and hit enter. Does this bring up any conversations that consist of one character asking another a ton of questions? If so, unless you're writing a courtroom scene, there's a strong chance you've found some on-the-nose dialogue.

2. The clear explanation test. Go through each conversation in the script and this time flag up each occasion a character explains something to another character in a very clear, rudimentary manner. Look out also for sudden announcements from characters about how they're feeling and explanations of how things work.

Now that you've potentially found some on-the-nose dialogue, what do you do about it? There are usually two possible solutions: "show don't tell" and "tell, but tell it with subtext." Let's start by taking a fresh look at the old cliche of "show don't tell."

THE POWER OF A VISUAL SCENE

On-the-nose dialogue is very often the result of characters simply expressing what they feel with words instead of through visual actions. In many cases the easiest way to combat clunky on-the-nose dialogue is to simply replace it with visual actions within a visual scene.

If we refer back to the scene between and Katie and Jennifer, it's a fairly typical example of a writer thinking verbally rather than visually. This results in Katie talking about actions and expressing emotions verbally, rather than showing us those actions and emotions visually.

Firstly, Jennifer asks Katie about the sitcom audition, but the script would be much better served by actually *showing us* Katie at the audition and how she screws it up. This would be a great opportunity to get some laughs in, put her under pressure, as well as show us her character. Remember: we learn much more about a character through their actions than their words. Seeing Katie leave the audition, sit down on a bench and start sobbing would tell us one thing about her.

Seeing her take a deep breath, put "Eye of the Tiger" on her iPod and strut down the street would tell us another.

Next, Jennifer asks Katie if she's going to take acting lessons and Katie explains she doesn't have any money. Instead, the writer could show us here how hard up Katie is by writing a scene in which she's out at dinner with friends and gets embarrassed when she has to order the cheapest meal on the menu.
Or we could see her car get towed and how she can't afford to get it back. Or her working overtime in Walmart, just to be able to go see her favorite band.

Jennifer then asks Katie if she's going to borrow some money from her parents. Again, this information could be shown instead of relayed through dialogue by having a visual scene in which, say, Katie accidentally writes off her mom's car and has to pay back thousands of dollars.

It's amazing also how once you start to replace dialogue with visual scenes— showing characters in action instead of just talking—a script starts to come alive. These visual scenes that replace conversations may all still contain dialogue, but the difference is that it'll be *supporting the scene* rather than carrying it.

For a real world example imagine if, in *La La Land*, we saw Mia sitting in a coffee shop complaining to a friend about how badly the audition went but didn't actually see her at the audition. Even if the new scene didn't contain any on-the-nose dialogue, it still wouldn't have been as interesting as the one in the film: Mia's visible pain and humiliation as the casting director answers a phone in the middle of her song.
Or imagine if, in *Sideways,* after Miles gets told by his agent

on the phone that his book isn't being published, we saw him go to straight to Jack and say, "I can't believe my book's not being published. I'm such a failure. I just want to go home," and so on. And imagine if this was followed up with Jack just talking to him, trying to cheer him up. The much more visually interesting (and funny) option is, of course, what's in the movie: Miles getting into an altercation with a pourer at the wine tasting, guzzling from the spit bucket and getting thrown out.

THE ART OF SUBTEXT

In many cases you may want to keep a conversation in the script rather than replace it with a visual scene. Which is great as well because there's much fun to be had crafting different layers into dialogue that are full of intensity and drama. But the key word here when writing these kind of conversations is "subtext."

It's simply impossible to write interesting dialogue without it, and is where the advice "what's *not* said is more important than what is said" comes in. But how do you take a stilted on-the-nose conversation and rewrite it to include all those deft layers of mysterious subtext? Let's refer back again to the scene between Katie and Jennifer. Injecting some subtext, emotion and depth into an on-the-nose conversation like this is actually fairly straightforward.

All that's required is simply taking a character's clear obvious explanation of something, or open expression of emotion, and replacing it with:

1. Words that hide the characters' true feelings
2. Words that subtly reveal to the audience what the characters already know

Let's take a look at both techniques using the dialogue in the sample scene.

HIDING EMOTIONS

Characters with real emotions don't talk like Katie and Jennifer. At the moment, their conversation feels lifeless and unrealistic because they're both laying all their emotional cards out on the table. In real life, however, people hide their vulnerabilities rather than explain everything they're feeling upfront. People use language as a tool to *disguise* what's really going on in their head, not explain it. They do everything in their power to hide their pain by skipping around things, edging around corners and trying to convince themselves and everyone else that they're fine.

If you've created characters who are damaged and flawed individuals, then it follows that their dialogue should also be damaged and flawed—i.e. deceptive. A lack of subtext, therefore, is often the result of underdeveloped characterizations, but we'll be addressing this later on in the book.

Take a look at this rewritten version of the sample scene in which this time Katie and Jennifer suppress their true feelings. Now Katie's hiding the fact her audition went terribly, and Jennifer's secretly glad that it did…

INT. KATIE'S BEDROOM - DAY

Katie and Jennifer are sitting on the bed.

                    JENNIFER
                    (stunned)
          You got a call back?

                    KATIE
          I did.

                    JENNIFER
          Wow, that's... cool.

                    KATIE
          They had me do the scene, sing a
          bit. I pretty much nailed it, so...

                    JENNIFER
          Who needs acting classes, right?

Katie shrugs.

This scene would still benefit from having previously shown Katie at the audition, but note how just by giving both characters some hidden emotions the dialogue's suddenly no longer on-the-nose.

Instead, the characters feel more human simply because now their words contradict what we know they're really feeling.

For a real world movie example, imagine if at the beginning of *Non-Stop*, after Bill gets talking to Jen on the plane, he comes right out and tells her, "My daughter's dead, actually. I still feel guilty about it because I wasn't there when she needed me, and now I'm an alcoholic."

This would, of course, feel ridiculously on-the-nose as opposed to what's actually in the film: Bill hiding his pain by talking about his daughter although she's still alive.

Or imagine if in *The Edge of Seventeen*, when Nadine asks Erwin on the ferris wheel to tell her something she doesn't know about him, he replied, "Well, I'm an amazing animator. I want a career doing animation for myself or for a studio, I haven't really made up my mind yet." Instead, he hides his talent from her, saying he's just a regular guy.

IMPLYING INFORMATION

Not every conversation, of course, will consist of characters hiding their true emotions. Sometimes they're totally up front with one another. In these cases on-the-nose dialogue can be avoided by making characters subtly imply things rather than explicitly announce them. Having characters *hint* at information feels more realistic because it means they've already discussed it—they know what they're talking about and so don't have to say things purely to keep the audience up to speed.

Here's another rewrite of the same scene using this technique—this time without the characters suppressing any hidden feelings or agendas:

INT. KATIE'S BEDROOM - DAY

Katie and Jennifer are sitting on the bed.

> JENNIFER
> Don't worry, something'll come up.

> KATIE
> When? I've been at this for three
> years and all I got to show for it
> is a cat food commercial.

> JENNIFER
> Maybe Carl can get you a discount
> at the studio.

> KATIE
> Does he accept sexual favors?

> JENNIFER
> Um, no...

> KATIE
> Yeah, well my mom's still on my case
> about her crappy Prius so I guess
> that idea's out.

In this case, Katie and Jennifer aren't hiding any emotions from each other, but they're talking in a much less "one plus one equals two" way because they're only hinting at background information rather than spelling it out. This requires trusting a bit more in your audience and that they'll be able to keep up. Once you strive to make them work a bit to figure out what's going on, the dialogue will automatically start to come alive.

HACK III: BUILD A "VOICE"

What's really meant by the ubiquitous advice to "give each character a voice" when it comes to dialogue? Here's a good way to get to grips with the concept: have a think about all the people you know and fictional characters you feel like you know in films. Start by thinking about all the members of your family, your friends and work colleagues. Now think about all the strangers you've met recently: the cab driver, teenage store clerk, teacher and so on. Finally, have a think about some protagonists from a few movies of your favorite movies: Sally Albright from *When Harry Met Sally*, Dirk Diggler from *Boogie Nights*, Whip Whitaker from *Flight*, or whoever they may be.

Now take a moment to consider just how different everyone's speech is, whether real or imaginary. Note how the way each person or character talks is defined by *who they are*: their experiences in life, personality, background, culture, profession, likes, dislikes and general outlook on the world. All of this comes together to make their words a reflection of what's important to them. In other words, it becomes their "voice."

Take a look at the dialogue-heavy opening to the movie, *Saw*. Here are two men of similar ages and in the same situation, and yet they have very different voices when it comes to their dialogue. This is because they have different views on the world, backgrounds, professions and ways of reacting to things. Consequently they speak differently too. And then

Jigsaw turns up and he speaks completely differently as well—choosing his words in a very careful and calculated manner.

In the film, *All The Money In The World*, there's a scene near the beginning in which John Paul Getty meets his son, daughter-in-law, Gail, and grandchild, Paul, for the first time in many years. However, he doesn't open with, "Come on in. It's been a long time hasn't it?" and then start talking about the weather.

He opens by talking about what's important to him: wealth, money and the value of material possessions:

GETTY
Dirty and old I have no problem
with at all. In fact I have some
affection for them as they're the
words most frequently used to
describe me, along with rich. But
priceless -- that's another thing
entirely. People say priceless when
what they really mean to say that
something is invaluable, or
irreplaceable. That Minotaur statuette
in your hands, for instance, dates
from 460BC; there are only a handful
like it remaining, and none in such
pristine condition. I'm sure those
fuckers at the Met or the British
Museum would kill to get their greasy
paws on it. Would you care to guess
what I paid for it?

This is another great example of creating dialogue that stands out based on the character's "voice." Getty's dialogue here is long-winded due to his self-absorbed, pompous and cold personality. He doesn't greet his family in a normal way at all. He has them stand there while he delivers this speech all about himself.

Every single character in your script should be defined in this way also. However, characters end up all sounding the same in a screenplay when the writer just gives them whatever dialogue they think they would say in the moment, without giving much thought to who they actually are and what's important to them.

The skill in writing killer dialogue, though, comes from finding your characters' voices within how they say and react to things in a certain way. You want to raise your dialogue to the level where, if each of your characters were sat down in front of a camera and asked to give their opinion on, say, religion, they'd each answer in a completely different way.

The first step to combatting the problem of characters sounding the same is to identify if it's actually happening in the first place. You've probably heard the advice to cover up all the names in your script and see if you can you tell the difference between their dialogue. This can be a good exercise, but the best way to identify the problem is to simply let other people read your script. If it exists, similar sounding dialogue will probably be one of the first comments a reader will make about the characters.

Assuming they're all tending to sound alike right now, what's the best way to tackle the problem?

MAKE YOUR CHARACTERS FEEL LIKE FAMILY

It's common in spec scripts to hear characters of different ages and from a variety of backgrounds and professions all speak the same way. Steve the policeman sounds exactly like Laura the neuroscientist. Margo the retired teacher talks just like Tommy the teenage jock. Carl the firefighter sounds exactly like Amy the heroin addict, and so on. The only way to stop all your characters sounding the same, though, is by giving each of them a "voice" and an independence on the page. And the only way to do that is to simply get to know them better.

The first thing you need to do is go through each characters' age, profession and background and make sure it really comes across in how they speak. How old are they? When we're sixty-four we tend to talk in a very different way to when we're twenty-four. Are your characters ages reflected in how they speak? Then ask yourself what each characters' job is and how much you know about it. How do people in their line of work generally talk? A New York cop, for example, should generally use a far more coarse and direct style of communication than a Californian yoga instructor.

Finally, what was their upbringing? Were they fending for themselves much of the time on the streets, or being pushed through an exclusive school by domineering parents. Again, all of this will feed into how they talk in the present day.

The next area to consider when giving each character a "voice" are their likes, dislikes and outlook on the world. Similarly, this requires taking each character in turn and considering what's most important to each one. If they had answer the question of what keeps them awake at night, what would they say? Are they the type of character who's idea of a perfect weekend is going kayaking down a river, or staying indoors watching wrestling? All of this should play into how they speak.

Once you have a good handle on each character's inner life, it's then just a case of doing a dialogue pass on the script and rewriting it to ensure every characters' words properly reflect what's important to them in the story and in life in general. There's a great Practical Exercise coming up in the next section that'll help you with this.

SUMMING UP

A final note on the rewrite process when it comes to dialogue: it's okay to write bad dialogue in a first draft. Don't go through the script first time around trying to make every characters' dialogue sound like it was written by Billy Wilder. This can be left for later rewrites in which you can really dive deep and make the dialogue come to life. By the end of any draft you should know a character ten times more that you did at the beginning and this, of course, will help you create dialogue that leaps off the page.

Doing a dialogue-only pass is a great idea, but it's one you want to save until the very end of a draft—once you're happy with the story, characters and theme. Then you can go back in and really sharpen up the dialogue, giving your characters those memorable lines that will make your script stand out above the rest.

PRACTICAL EXERCISES

"I was kind of excited about going to jail the first time—I learnt some great dialogue."
– Quentin Tarantino

Now we get to the fun part: three practical exercises that will really help you get into the nuts and bolts of how to write dialogue like the pros.

(Note: We haven't included the advice to read your dialogue aloud as we're kind of taking that as a given. Everyone knows that advice, and so just make sure you keep it up while adding in the exercises below.)

EXERCISE I: REFORMAT TRANSCRIPTIONS

An abundance of dialogue in a scene—specifically chit-chat between characters about events in the past or the future—often means the whole scene needs to be reworked or cut. This is usually a symptom of not first making absolutely sure each scene serves a purpose. But, presuming you're working on a scene that deserves to be in the screenplay, here's an exercise to stop overwriting dialogue when one line (or no line) would do:

The general advice is to, "cut as much dialogue as you can," "keep the dialogue to three lines or less," and of course, "show don't tell." But this can be hard to do if the fantastic argument between Josh and Francesco that you've just sweated over for three days reads perfectly well in your head. Stepping outside your head and seeing the dialogue objectively can be really difficult, and that's why the "just cut the dialogue" theory might make sense intellectually, but still often goes unheeded.

Here's an exercise that will force you into writing short, tight, flowing lines of dialogue. Firstly, pick a movie from the Resources Toolkit in the next section, called 25 Transcriptions To Reformat, and watch it.
Even if you know it, watch it again as this will freshen it up in your mind and make the exercise easier. Next, copy and paste the transcript of the movie into your favored screenplay software. It will come out all messed up but that's okay. Now it's time to go through the entire document and reformat all the dialogue so it's back in shape. It's as simple as that. Go through the character names, parentheticals and dialogue, and put everything in its right place. You don't have to worry about scene description, just focus on the dialogue, making sure it's all correctly formatted.

F. Scott Fitzgerald used to do a similar exercise but with novels. He'd take a book he admired and type it out word for word on his typewriter, just to get into the rhythm of the prose. It's really cool how doing this feeds into your own writing consciousness. Through reformatting scene after scene of professional screenplays, your fingers will naturally begin to fall into the rhythm of writing more professional sounding dialogue. It'll become lean and direct, rather than flabby and bloated, and it'll also give it a more natural "flow." In fact, this exercise is so good it should be done by every screenwriter wishing to improve his or her dialogue whether it suffers from overwriting or not. It does require a fair amount of effort, but the rewards are tremendous.

Note: some writers choose to reformat transcriptions from a variety of genres. It is entirely up to you but we find that writers benefit more from transcribing dialogue from their chosen genre. If you stick to the one you want to write in while doing these exercises, it will make it easier to get into the rhythm of writing the dialogue for that particular genre. Say you're a Comedy writer, it'll be so much more beneficial to reformat to reformat five Comedies than three Horrors, a Comedy and a Thriller. And remember—you should be reformatting many more than five movies. Just head on over to an online script database like *Drew's Script-o-Rama* and dive in. The more you do the better.

EXERCISE II: REWRITE AMATEUR DIALOGUE

Sometimes, even after all that dialogue has been cut to short, snappy lines surrounded by a ton of white space, it can still feel on-the-nose, unnatural and unexciting. Nothing wants to make a reader want to put their head in an oven faster than a tension-free Q&A style conversation between Mandy and Jason about her new job. So, just how do you eliminate the scourge of on-the-nose dialogue in a practical way?

Here's the exercise: Go to the 5 Amateur Dialogue Scenes section in the Resources Toolkit, and rewrite the dialogue. The first thing you should do when considering the scene (or dialogue in this case) is decide on what you want it to reveal to the audience. This has already been done for you, as each one has a heading describing what the purpose of the scene is. Next, brainstorm some different ways the conversation could play out, and then write a quick version of the same scene. Don't just go with the first thing that pops into your head as this will invariably be the least interesting.

For example, imagine two versions of the following scene: Anna has to tell a neighbor who's just returned from vacation that while he was away she accidentally ran over his cat, and now it's in intensive care at the local animal hospital.

1. Here's an amateur screenwriter version. Anna knocks on the neighbor's door and tells him she ran over the cat. He flips out. She apologizes. He asks her a million questions. She offers to drive him to the animal hospital. They jump in her car and drive off.

2. Here's a better version. Anna knocks on the door and starts talking about *anything but* the injured cat—the pesky neighborhood kids, the hot weather, the neighbor's trip—and the scene ends with him asking, "Where's Smokey by the way?" CUT TO: Anna driving the furious neighbor to the animal hospital.

Aspiring screenwriters will often default to the more obvious dialogue in the first version, but the second version acquired after a little brainstorming is obviously the more interesting one.

We've added some brainstorm ideas at the end of each scene to get your creative juices flowing. Finally, add some structure to the dialogue. Make sure the scene has a Set Up, Call to Action, Act 1 Turning Point, etc. sculpted by the conversation. You can find out more about this in the link provided in the Resources Toolkit in the next section. To practice some more, get hold of a few unproduced, spec screenplays in your chosen genre and rewrite five, ten, twenty more scenes.

EXERCISE III: GET TO KNOW YOUR CHARACTERS

Aspiring screenwriters are often told that all their characters sound the same. The grandma sounds the same as the teenager. The professor sounds the same as the stripper, etc. The advice generally given to remedy this problem is to, "give each character a unique voice, speech patterns, inflections, and vocabulary," And/or, "give each one a favorite subject they always reference." There are also a few practical exercises designed to help this, such as, "cover up the names to see how easy it is to tell who's speaking," and, "go out and secretly record the flow of how people speak in real life."

Writers will then spend a day or two hanging around Starbucks eavesdropping on some random conversations, all the while wondering what they're supposed to be listening for. Then they'll go home and add an idiosyncratic lisp to one character's dialogue, a fondness for burping to another's, and a constant reference to *Star Wars* movies to another's. None of which gets them very far because the real reason all their characters sound the same is that they haven't yet figured out who each character really is.

What differentiates most character's dialogue is not *how* they speak—quickly, slowly, with a lisp, a drawl, a stutter—but what they say and the attitude behind it. If you go ahead and cover up the names for Carrie, Miranda, Charlotte and Samantha in a *Sex and the City* script, can you really tell who's speaking by their different dialogue patterns and "flow"? No. They're all successful women living in New York of around the same age and without any noticeable speech impediments. But you can tell whose dialogue is whose by what they say and the attitude that comes out through their words.

There are two parts to this exercise.

PART I

Get to know each character on a much deeper level than you do already. Start by making a list of all the major and minor characters in your screenplay and then, underneath each name, write down some key facts: their age, profession/life status, likes, dislikes, personality traits, etc.
Refer back to their overriding, obvious personality trait and their contradictory trait. (See the link to, Why Creating A Character Bio Isn't A Good Idea And What You Should Do Instead, in the Resources Toolkit for more information on this.) Add more traits to the list—whatever you think best sums up this character. Then it's just a question of making sure each character expresses the elements of the personality—their brashness, diffidence, prudence, sexuality, intelligence, dumbness, and so on—through what they say.

Focus on what they choose to talk about, what they dwell on and how they react in different situations. Once each character is doing this in a different way from every other character, their individual personalities will begin to shine through. In later drafts you can also highlight each characters' name using Cmd + F and check their dialogue remains true to their personality all the way through the screenplay.

PART II

Here's part two of the exercise: in-field research. You may be able to accurately imagine how a soccer mom, shop assistant or teacher talks because you probably come into contact with these kind of people all the time. But what about FBI agents, pole dancers, professional skateboarders or Russian hitmen? Chances are you'll have less contact with the second group, and so here's where some in-field research comes in handy. If one of your main characters is a professor of ethics at NYU, do some investigating to find out how professors actually talk. If you can't get ready access to a skatepark to hang around and eavesdrop, or don't particularly feel like flying to Moscow to hang out with the Russian mafia, watch videos about them on YouTube. Read interviews. Read novels. Immerse yourself in the language of the Los Angeles skate scene or the Russian underworld and you'll make not only make your characters' dialogue 100 percent more believable, but their personalities overall.

RESOURCES TOOLKIT

"When I act, I hear it like music. In my head, I hear the dialogue like music."
– Nicolas Cage

In this section you'll find information on how to format dialogue to industry standard, transcriptions to reformat, examples of bad dialogue to rewrite, and suggested further reading.

PART I: HOW TO FORMAT DIALOGUE

Some writers like to cut corners by using free or cheap software, or even in MS Word (ouch). If you want to be a screenwriter, though, you'll need to bite the bullet and purchase some professional software if you haven't already. Final Draft and Movie Magic are the two leading brands right now, but Fade In is a great cheaper alternative.

Writing dialogue using professional software takes all the heavy lifting out of the formatting process, as everything is pre-set to industry standards right out of the box. However, there are still a number of elements when it comes to formatting dialogue that can cause confusion or get overlooked whether you're using professional software or not. Let's start with the basics:

Screenplay dialogue consists of just three elements:

1. Character name. The name of who's speaking, written in uppercase.

2. Actor direction. A cue to the actor in brackets under the name, telling them to perform a particular action or covey a particular emotion.

3. Character dialogue. The actual words delivered by the actor.

Let's take a look at each element in more detail and the common mistakes often found in each that you should avoid.

CHARACTER NAME

The first element is the character name—also known as the character cue, character slug and character caption. Here are the correct margins for the character name: 3.7 inches from left side of page (2.2 inches from margin.)

It may sound obvious but the most important thing to remember when it comes to character names is to keep them short and consistent throughout the script. Generally, first names only are used. Write DARREN rather than DARREN FITZGERALD. Similarly, if you introduce a character as CAPTAIN LYNCH, he should stay as CAPTAIN LYNCH, rather than alternate between CAPTAIN CLIFF LYNCH, CAPT. LYNCH, and LYNCH. All are acceptable but the key is consistency.

It doesn't happen often, but let's say you want to have a character enter a scene, but only introduce them later on in that scene. In this case, it can be handled like so:

A FEMALE HIPSTER enters the party and surveys the scene. She stops a passing DUDE.

                    FEMALE HIPSTER
              Hey, you seen Lisa?

Let's say later on in the scene you want us know what her name is, it can be done like this:

                    TOMMY
              Frances! You made it.

               FRANCES (FEMALE HIPSTER)
              Unfortunately, yeah.

Frances lights a cigarette.

                    FRANCES
              Look, I'm not here to play games.
              Where is she?

Once it's been established that the Female Hipster is Frances, you can lose the brackets.

On the other hand, if we hear a character's voice before seeing them, it can be handled like this:

Kevin stumbles off the side of the road.

                    MAN'S VOICE (O.S.)
              It's so much better on the other side...
Kevin turns to see GERALD BROOKS, dressed in a white robe, calmly levitating a few feet off the ground.

                        GERALD
                  ... we get free parking.

Now let's take a look at what to do if you have multiple
characters all speaking at once, or in rapid succession.

If you just have two characters speaking at the same time you
can use the dual dialogue feature in your screenwriting
software. But let's say you have a scene in which a group of
angry protestors have set up camp outside the White House,
all speaking quickly, one after the other. The most common
solution is to give them individual lines and number their
character names, like this:

                      PROTESTOR #1
                  Silence is violence!

                      PROTESTOR #2
              We reject the president elect!

                      PROTESTOR #3
            Love not hate makes America great!

Writing PROTESTOR 1, PROTESTOR ONE, and FIRST
PROTESTOR would also be an option. There are no steadfast
rules here other than it's important to remain consistent.
Another option would be to simply write PROTESTORS as a
group name and then add their dialogue like this:

                      PROTESTORS
                  Silence is violence!/We reject the
                  president elect!/Love not hate makes
                  America great!

Sometimes one of three optional cues directly follow a character name: VOICE OVER (V.O.), OFF-SCREEN (O.S.), and CONTINUED (CONT'D).

VOICE OVER and OFF-SCREEN seem to sometimes cause a great deal of confusion, but here's an easy way to tell the difference. VOICE OVER is used whenever we hear a character's voice, but they're not physically in the scene's location—*they're somewhere else entirely*. Examples would be:

1. Narrating events
2. On the other end of a phone
3. On a TV, computer screen or radio
4. On a loudspeaker
5. On an answering machine or tape recording
6. Overlapping voices from the previous or following scene
7. Memories, hallucinations, or imagination

Here's how they're implemented:

Amy tentatively picks up her phone and hits "call."

> ZACH (V.O.)
> Hello?

> AMY
> Hi, Zach? It's Amy.

> ZACH (V.O.)
> Amy who?

VOICE OVER always gets written in uppercase, enclosed by brackets and with a period space between the last letter of the character name and the first bracket. It doesn't look like any of these:

1. ZACH VO
2. ZACH V.O.
3. ZACH (VO)
4. ZACH (v.o.)
5. ZACH(V.O.)

OFF-SCREEN, on the other hand, is used when a character is just that—off-screen, but not in a completely different location. They're in the vicinity of the scene, *but out of view*. A few examples would be characters who are:

1. In another room
2. Talking before entering a scene
3. Behind a secret bookcase

Here's an example:

INT. BOEING 747 (FLYING) - DAY

Lauren lurches toward the cockpit door as the plane violently rolls from left to right. She raps on the door.

                    LAUREN
          Captain?! What's happening?

                    CAPTAIN FARBER (O.S.)
          Lauren -- ask the passengers if anyone
          knows how to land a plane!

Just as with VOICE OVER, it's important to stick to the correct formatting: all uppercase and with no irregular spacing, lack of periods, or brackets. OFF-CAMERA (O.C.) can also used but it's generally only employed in TV scripts.

CONTINUED (CONT'D) also causes quite a bit of confusion because some screenwriting gurus insist it has to be used, while others say it's old fashioned and should never be seen in a screenplay. Most screenwriting programs, however, automatically insert a (CONT'D) after a character's name whenever their dialogue is interrupted by description, like this:

Harvey ducks down behind a boulder.

HARVEY
Ben, stay back!

Ben crawls toward him on all fours as BULLETS whizz overhead.

HARVEY (CONT'D)
Ben! I said stay back!

Our advice is to just be consistent. If you use them, keep them in. If not, keep them out. (The one place they are mandatory is in a multi-camera TV script.)

ACTOR DIRECTION

The second element that makes up dialogue are the actor directions—also known as parentheticals, personal directions and wrylies. Here are the correct margins for actor directions:

3.1 inches from left side of page (1.6 from margin).

The biggest mistake we see when it comes to parentheticals is simply using too many of them. If you have an actor direction on every other page of the script, you're overusing them. They should only be used *very sparingly* in the following three circumstances, when:

1. A character's words need clarifying
2. It's not clear who or what a character's referring to
3. A character performs a small action

Here's an example of the first and most common use of actor directions—when their words need clarifying:

> ASTRID
> (sarcastically)
> You're so right, Lucas.

In this case, the actor playing Astrid might not know that she's being sarcastic based solely on her words and so an actor direction clears this up nicely.

Problems arise, however, when they get added even though it's clear what the character's intent is, like in this example:

> TINA
> (shocked)
> I can't believe you just said that.

> CURTIS
> (angrily)
> Get out and don't come back!

These actor directions are just redundant and so make sure you only use them when absolutely necessary.

There are also a few standard actor directions to bear in mind, though. Firstly, if a character's speaking in a foreign language and you want the audience to be able to understand them, you can write "subtitled" in an actor direction, like this:

> GENNARO
> (in Italian, subtitled)
> Pass me the ball, Ricardo.

However, if the characters speak in a foreign language for more than a couple of lines or a whole scene, it's better to indicate it up front:

The two women sit down on the edge of the pier. They speak in Danish, SUBTITLED:

> FREJA
> How long do you think you'll stay?

> ANNA
> As long as I have to.

It can also be helpful to write END SUBTITLES at the end of a scene spoken in a foreign language, just to make it clear we're back to English.

The second standard actor direction is the much-overused "beat." Again, it should be used sparingly, not like in the example below:

                    LANA
          I've never seen this movie in my
          life.
                    (beat)
          No, wait.
                    (beat)
          Doesn't this guy wind up homeless at
          the end?

(The term "beat" can also be switched out for "long beat,"
"short beat," and "then.")

Another situation in which actor directions can help clear up
confusion, is if you have three or more characters in a scene
and it isn't clear who's talking to who:

                    MATT
          You walk in dressed like that and
          I'm the idiot?

                    OWEN
          You always have to ruin everything.

                    KATE
                    (to Matt)
          How about I drive you home?

Or, sometimes you want to make it clear that a character's
referring to something specific. In this case, the term "re:" is
used.

Iggy paces as Saul collapses in his Lazy-Boy and sighs.

> SAUL
> (re: Iggy's pants)
> You might want to change those.

On some occasions it's simpler to state a small character action in an actor direction rather than in a line of description:

> RAPHAEL
> (yawning)
> I am so pumped to go see this play.

Be careful in these instances to not overdo the descriptions, though. The following, for example, would be incorrect:

> VERONICA
> (taking a long puff on a
> cigarette and blowing a big
> smoke ring into the air)
> Your deal.

Overall, it's important to remember to keep actor directions to a minimum and in the correct format. This means an actor description should never:

1. Be capitalized at the beginning
2. Have a period at the end (apart from an occasional exclamation mark)
3. Hang alone underneath dialogue
4. Describe actions made by another character
5. Start with "he" or "she"

CHARACTER DIALOGUE

Here are the correct margins for character dialogue: 2.5 inches from left side of page (1.5 from margin). Below you'll find a number of formatting "rules" that you should bear in mind while writing dialogue. While none of them are going to get you a "pass" grade on their own, a blatant disregard for these conventions won't endear your dialogue to anyone reading it.

1. Emphasized words. If you want a character to emphasize a particular word, it's general practice to underline it, rather than use italics or bold. Some writers use uppercase instead, but whatever you do, don't go crazy emphasizing words on every page. As usual: *use sparingly.*

2. Numbers. Where possible spell out numbers in dialogue as writing numerals often looks ungainly on the page and can be awkward for actors to read. For example, write, "I've been here twenty times and still get lost," not, "I've been here 20 times and still get lost." Exceptions are when it comes to dates, phone numbers and codes. In these cases write, "It's May 30th, 1966. The phone number is 212-333-2206 and the password is Circa1762." However, you should never start a line with a numeral. "8 rounds were fired, sir," should be "Eight rounds were fired, sir."

3. Ellipses and dashes. Use these to give the dialogue a more realistic feel but, again, don't overdo it. Using an ellipsis is a great to show a character trailing off in thought or pausing, and should always be three periods long. Not two. Not four, but three: "Oh my god..." Dashes, on the other hand, indicate a sudden break or shift in the character's words and are always written by typing a space, followed by hyphen, hyphen, followed by another space. They're a good way of showing a character get interrupted, like this: "I thought he was -- " "Well he wasn't!" (In this case, there's no need to add "interrupted" as an actor direction as well.)

4. Initials and acronyms. The general rule here is to place periods in-between confusing or unknown initials and acronyms to make it clear each letter has to be spoken separately, like this: "All you have to do is connect the G.A.T. to the X.R-4 and then loop through the J.O.P." If they're initials or acronyms in everyday use, though, such as, NFL, NBC, Navy SEAL, etc. then it's not so important.

5. Accents and colloquialisms. Depending on the character, having them speak in a grammatically incorrect manner can really help bring their dialogue to life. It's perfectly fine to write, "Jeez, boy, git outta my way! I ain't gonna warn ya again," or, "Well, helloooo there, tiger." However, be very, *very* careful not to overdo this either. Use these inflections judiciously to enhance character, rather than giving each one a different set of colloquialisms, or peppering their dialogue with words like, "Mariaaaaaaa!" "Stoooooop!" "Fiiiiirrreeeee!"

6. Telephone and online conversations. The most important thing to consider here is, can we see both characters or just one? If we can only see one you'll need to add a VOICE OVER cue beside the other *unseen* character's name. If we can see both, because you're intercutting between locations, then this isn't needed. See the link to the formatting phone calls post in the Dig Deeper section below for a more detailed analysis of this.

7. Song lyrics. If a character sings in your script, the easiest solution is to add the actor direction (singing) and then format their dialogue normally but using quotation marks, like so:

"You're the top. You're Mahatma Gandhi. You're the top. You're Napoleon Brandy." Some professional writers like to put song lyrics in italics, or end each line with a slash "/" but we think simple quotes look neater on the page. Note: if you're writing an actual musical there's a whole different set of rules you need to follow: lyrics are justified left and in uppercase. Final Draft and Movie Magic have templates for this built into the program that you can check out.

PART II: 25 TRANSCRIPTIONS TO REFORMAT

Here are twenty-five screenplays that have been transcribed from the movie. Simply copy and paste them into your screenwriting software and reformat the dialogue as discussed in Exercise I of the Practical Exercises section.

DRAMA

Almost Famous
http://www.script-o-rama.com/movie_scripts/a/almost-famous-script-transcript-crudup.html

Boogie Nights
http://www.script-o-rama.com/movie_scripts/b/boogie-nights-script-transcript.html

Monster's Ball
http://www.script-o-rama.com/movie_scripts/m/monsters-ball-script-transcript-halle.html

The People Vs. Larry Flynt
http://www.script-o-rama.com/movie_scripts/p/people-vs-larry-flynt-script.html

The Virgin Suicides
http://www.script-o-rama.com/movie_scripts/v/virgin-suicides-script-transcript.html

COMEDY

The 40 Year Old Virgin
http://www.script-o-rama.com/movie_scripts/f/40-year-old-virgin-script.html

The Hangover
http://www.script-o-rama.com/movie_scripts/h/the-hangover-script-transcript.html

Legally Blonde
http://www.script-o-rama.com/movie_scripts/l/legally-blonde-script-transcript-reese.html

Manhattan
http://www.script-o-rama.com/movie_scripts/m/manhattan-script-transcript-woody-allen.html

Mean Girls
http://www.script-o-rama.com/movie_scripts/mean-girls-movie-transcript.html

ACTION/ADVENTURE

The Bourne Identity
http://www.script-o-rama.com/movie_scripts/b/bourne-identity-script-transcript-damon.html

Catch Me If You Can
http://www.script-o-rama.com/movie_scripts/c/catch-me-if-you-can-script.html

Con Air
http://www.script-o-rama.com/movie_scripts/c/con-air-script-transcript.html

Kill Bill
http://www.script-o-rama.com/movie_scripts/k/kill-bill-script-transcript-uma.html

Men In Black
http://www.script-o-rama.com/movie_scripts/m/men-in-black-script-transcript.html

THRILLER

Enemy Of The State
http://www.script-o-rama.com/movie_scripts/e/enemy-of-the-state-script.html

Fargo
http://www.script-o-rama.com/movie_scripts/f/fargo-script-transcript-coen.html

Gone Baby Gone
http://www.script-o-rama.com/movie_scripts/g/gone-baby-gone-script-transcript.html

Identity
http://www.script-o-rama.com/movie_scripts/i/identity-script-transcript-john-cusack.html

The Machinist
http://www.script-o-rama.com/movie_scripts/m/machinist-script-transcript-christian-bale.html

HORROR

Dawn Of The Dead
http://www.script-o-rama.com/movie_scripts/d/dawn-of-the-dead-script-transcript.html

The Exorcism Of Emily Rose
http://www.script-o-rama.com/movie_scripts/e/exorcism-of-emily-rose-script.html

The Grudge
http://www.script-o-rama.com/movie_scripts/g/grudge-script-transcript-remake-gellar.html

I Know What You Did Last Summer
http://www.script-o-rama.com/movie_scripts/i/i-know-what-you-did-last-summer-script.html

The Shining
http://www.script-o-rama.com/movie_scripts/s/shining-script-transcript-jack-nicholson.html

PART III: 5 AMATEUR DIALOGUE EXAMPLES

A great way to improve your own dialogue is by rewriting badly written dialogue as it helps you more easily step back from your own work and recognize its faults. Below you'll find five scenes from real spec scripts that contain all the major dialogue mistakes we've discussed in this book: overwritten conversations, on-the-nose dialogue and characters who all sound the same.

Use these scenes to get you started but also seek out spec scripts from aspiring writers and read as many as you can. Just like professional screenplays, they'll teach you *a lot*.

SCENE I: BOY MEETS GIRL

Eric, a young volunteer in the Peace Corps, has recently

arrived for another stint in Africa. Here he meets a new, attractive volunteer named Diana. They've seen each other around but not spoken yet, until now...

EXT — ERIC'S HUT — MORNING

Eric works in his garden with his shirt off and MUSIC playing on an old stereo system. Diana arrives on a bike. She drinks in a fast glance of his chest.

> DIANA
> Hi, neighbor.

> ERIC
> You're moving in next door?

> DIANA
> Yep, just got the word.

They shake hands.

> ERIC
> Damn, that's a hardy handshake you
> have there.
> DIANA
> Country girl you know.

> ERIC
> I think I'll stick with hugs from
> now on. Welcome to my, soon to be
> our, little slice of heaven.

Diana inspects her hut.

ERIC (CONT'D)

Hey, as far as the move, give me a
time when you think you might start
and if I can help you in any way that
doesn't inconvenience me in any way,
please let me know.

DIANA

Is that sarcasm I hear?

ERIC

No, lord no, sarcasm's meant to wound
or ridicule, or something like that.
Your addition to this little patch of
suburbia bush jungle is a real plus.
Now, on the other hand, if I had said,
for instance, there goes the neighborhood, that might have been a good
sarcastic, yet sadly predictable thing
to say.

DIANA

Are you always so up and full of
funny? You sure seem to be.

ERIC

Ears of the beholder. Ears of the
beholder. Anyway, as far as I can
tell, the whole world laughs in the
same language so why not?

Eric freezes.

> ERIC (CONT'D)
> Where the hell are my manners? Let
> me get you a beer.

He turns toward his hut and gets one.

> ERIC (CONT'D)
> These beers are remarkably cool for
> their vintage.

> DIANA
> It's not even ten! Maybe one or two
> on moving day. See you then? I'm off
> to the guesthouse to start packing so
> I can unpack again.

She rides off.

> ERIC
> (calls after her)
> I don't really drink beer until well
> after noon — unless, of course, it's
> offered to me, and it's free. I'm very
> disciplined in that way. Oh and it wasn't
> really humor, it was wit. I'm witty.

BRAINSTORM TIME

Now it's time to brainstorm and rewrite the scene, finding a much more interesting way into it. What funny thing might Eric (or Diana) do to totally mess up this promising situation? What could Diana already know about him and not let on? What kind of playful interaction using innuendo or metaphor could they engage in?

SCENE II: THE CONFESSION

Simon has just been unexpectedly fired from his corporate job without a reason and without severance. His wife, Annabel, knows he's lost his job but doesn't know he won't be getting paid.

INT. DINING ROOM — NIGHT

Simon and Annabel eat dinner. Simon has a little more food, but not like his normal appetite.

> ANNABEL
> I was thinking about our finances.
> How much did you get for severance?

> SIMON
> Nothing. It's not a law.

> ANNABEL
> Are you sure?

> SIMON
> Yes.

> ANNABEL

That doesn't seem possible after ten
years. Who would do that?

        SIMON
I know. It is so wrong.

        ANNABEL
Williams Broadcasting is so corrupt
with their greed. Money is God,
what a laugh! As long as they treat
people so badly, they'll never
be truly successful, until they
learn people are their most
valuable asset.

        SIMON
Those super bad idiots.

        ANNABEL
We keep our medical insurance under
your plan, with the state program right?

        SIMON
I saw the figures. We would have to
pay 102 percent now. Premiums that are outta
this world. We won't be able to afford
it on my unemployment insurance, only
about half of my normal wage.

Annabel is stunned.

BRAINSTORM TIME

How could the question of money come up in a casual conversation—like an expensive school trip for one of their kids—which then leads to Simon's revelation that he didn't get any severance pay? Or what might Simon's strategy be to broach the difficult subject of his not getting any money? How might Annabel completely freak out, revealing a side to her character we didn't know existed?

SCENE III: THE TRICK

Three teenage girls, Eva, Tamara and Laura are having a party (their parents are out). But when it comes time to leave one of them impersonates her mom and rings another mom, trying to win them a sleepover.

INT. LOUNGE — NIGHT

The girls have just finished watching TV.

> EVA
> We should get going.

> TAMARA
> Unless...

> EVA
> Unless what?

> TAMARA
> Laura could pretend to be your mom

and phone our parents to ask if we
could have a sleep over.

                    EVA
Great idea, Laura is wicked at
impersonating Mrs. Jackson.

                  TAMARA
Please, Laura.

Laura nods and reaches for the phone.

                  LAURA
Hi Sarah, it's Pat.

                SARAH (V.O.)
Pat, your voice sounds strange.

Laura coughs and clears throat.

                  LAURA
Yes, I have had laryngitis.

                SARAH (V.O.)
Oh no, you poor thing send the children
home if you are feeling unwell.

                  LAURA
No not at all, they are playing nicely.
In fact, I was wondering if they would
like to stay the night.

> SARAH (V.O.)
> What is the occasion?

> LAURA
> The occasion... Erm, it's national be
> kind to your neighbors day.

> SARAH (V.O.)
> Really?! Wow, that's fantastic. George
> and I could do with a break.

Laura hangs up, then all hell lets loose. Loud MUSIC, dancing, pillow fights.

BRAINSTORM TIME

What could the kids be doing that's so amazing they don't want to go home? How could they trick Sarah over the phone in a more interesting way than how it's written? How might their plan backfire so we think they've been found out?

SCENE IV: YOU HAVE TO BELIEVE ME

Robert is convinced his father didn't hang himself but is in fact the victim of the Suicide Kid—a serial killer who makes all his victims look like they killed themselves. Trouble is, Robert's having a hard time persuading the cop, Edwin, of his theory.

INT. POLICE STATION — NIGHT

Edwin is striding down the hall, a folder in his hand. Robert catches up to him.

                    ROBERT
          This is my dad we're talking about.

                    EDWIN
          Which changes nothing about the fact
          that he hung himself.

                    ROBERT
          But that can't be right...

                    EDWIN
          Sometimes, you just don't feel like

          living anymore, and believe me kid, he
          stopped living a long time ago.

Edwin picks up two donuts lying in a box on a counter that he
whizzes by.

                    ROBERT
          What if he was murdered, huh?? What if
          all they say about the Suicide Kid is
          true? The landlady, her husband died in
          the same way!

                    EDWIN
          Ha! Anytime anyone trips over a shoe
          lace or sneezes too much in this town,
          people think that gives them an excuse
          to play detective and throw the Suicide

Kid's name around. They don't know what
they're doing and neither do you.

                    ROBERT
          But this is my dad!

                    EDWIN
          With all due respect, you might want to
          stop saying that in public.

                    ROBERT
          What?

Edwin stops.

                    EDWIN
          Listen Rob, I don't know what your
          deal is, but there is no record of
          Brad James ever having a son. Whatever
          kind of crazy you are, you're not going
          to be the kind that wastes my time.

Robert is stunned.

                    ROBERT
          H-how can you even... say that? I mean...
          he taught me everything, he taught me
          how to write --

                    EDWIN
          Jeff! Drive Sherlock home will ya?

Edwin opens the door to the front entrance where the ROAR

of the media frenzy can be heard and exits. Robert is gutted.

BRAINSTORM TIME

Where might this scene take place other than a police station to give the dialogue a different feel? What desperate measure could Robert take to try and convince Edwin? What evidence could reveal itself here to push the story forward?

SCENE V: THE DEAL

Linda has only just joined Valerie's real estate firm a week ago but has already closed her first big deal.

INT. REALTOR COMPANY — DAY

Valerie and Linda walk out of the office and into the hallway.

> VALERIE
> Well Linda, how did that feel?

> LINDA
> How did what feel?

> VALERIE
> Your first closing? Didn't that feel
> great?

> LINDA
> Yes it did! Thanks for letting me
> join your office. You've taught me so
> much. I just hope I'm prepared. My

uncle is almost finished with his
Brentwood condo project!

Linda stops and turns to Valerie.

> LINDA (CONT'D)
> Do you realize that I will be the
> Listing Agent for thirty-nine luxury
> condos? Me? Linda Moss? Can you
> believe it?

Valerie loops her left arm around Linda's neck and smiles.

> VALERIE
> Oh, you better believe I do!

> LINDA
> How about, "Linda Moss, Realtor for
> the Stars."

> VALERIE
> That's my line, dear.

> LINDA
> Oh, right.

BRAINSTORM TIME

How might Valerie lead us to think she's faking her joy at
Linda's success? Why might Linda be afraid to tell Valerie
she's just secured the deal? What could Valerie reveal about
the job that puts a huge damper on Linda's enthusiasm?

PART IV: DIG DEEPER

You'll find a short list of blog posts and resources on dialogue, character and formatting below to help further develop your dialogue skills:

1. Take Acting Classes. If you're struggling with writing dialogue one of the very best ways you can improve it is by joining an acting class and putting yourself directly in the actors' shoes when it comes to interpreting dialogue. Jump on CraigsList or Meetup.com as a starting point and pop in your local city.

2. Organize A Table Read. Similarly, rather than just reading your dialogue aloud to yourself, get some people together and do a table read. Stage32 is a great place to meet like-minded writers and there's also a contest in which you can win a table read:
https://tablereadmyscreenplay.com

3. How To Write A Phone Conversation In A Screenplay. Confused by how to format a telephone call in a screenplay? This guide will explain all you need to know:
http://www.scriptreaderpro.com/write-phone-conversation-screenplay/

4. How To Write Comedy Scripts With LOL Dialogue. This post contains a great hack for writing funny dialogue that applies to all scripts, whether you're writing a Comedy or not:
http://www.scriptreaderpro.com/how-to-write-comedy-scripts/

5. 50 Of The Best Screenplays To Read And Download In Every Genre. Reading scripts is probably the best way to learn how to write dialogue. These fifty are the perfect

introduction:
http://www.scriptreaderpro.com/best-screenplays-to-read/

6. Why Creating A Character Bio Isn't A Good Starting Point. This post contains a cool little two-step process you can use when trying to create realistic characters:
http://www.scriptreaderpro.com/character-bio/

7. The 8 Dramatic Principles Of Writing A Scene. Discover the eight core principles you should follow when writing a scene in order to keep the audience engaged and move the story forward:
http://www.scriptreaderpro.com/screenplay-scene/

OUTRO

"If it sounds like writing, I rewrite it."
– Elmore Leonard

Thank you once again for purchasing and reading this book. We hope it's helped clear up some of the confusion and mystery out there surrounding how to write effective dialogue. Follow the steps outlined in this book and you should soon feel like you're much more in control over your characters, and how what they say reflects who they are.

Finally, don't forget it's important that a spec script contains a couple of those "movie lines" that people love to quote. The stuff that goes on a t-shirt. The "fasten your seatbelts, it's going to be a bumpy night," "you're gonna need a bigger boat," and "you talkin' to me?" lines that will make an actor kill to play the role. This is definitely not something that's easy to do but it's important to remember that, as well as being functional, dialogue needs to be *memorable*.

As a quick recap, here are the practical steps you can take every day to master screenplay dialogue and get it up to a professional level:

1. Make your dialogue sharper and more concise by reformatting transcriptions. Pick a transcription from the Resources Toolkit, put it into your own screenwriting software and simply reformat it so it looks like a proper screenplay. This is an invaluable exercise.

2. Eliminate bad dialogue by rewriting badly written scenes. Rewrite all five scenes in the Resources Toolkit and then continue the practice by reading as many spec scripts as you can and noting how you would've written the scene yourself.

3. Stop characters from sounding the same by really getting to know them. Write lists of each of their character traits and use this to make sure they always say what they would say in any given situation. Do in-field research to figure out how the less obvious characters speak.

4. Read professional screenplays. Follow the link to the 50 Of The Best Screenplays To Read And Download In Every Genre post and get reading. Your writing routine should include reading at least two screenplays a week.

5. Read dialogue out loud. Organize a table read of your script with friends, join an acting class, and read your own dialogue out loud to yourself as you write. Always remember: dialogue in a screenplay differs from dialogue in a novel in this one key respect—it's designed to be performed.

If you liked this book and found it helpful, we'd be eternally grateful if you could help spread the word!

You can do that via Facebook:
www.facebook.com/pg/scriptreaderpro/reviews

And don't hesitate to <u>contact us</u> if you have any questions regarding the concepts surrounding dialogue discussed in this book, or want to make any suggestions or comments.

Thanks again for taking the time to read this book. We look forward to reading your characters' rocking dialogue. :)

Happy writing,
Alex & the Script Reader Pro team
www.scriptreaderpro.com
You write. We Read. They Love

Printed in Great Britain
by Amazon

46682356R10043